We Bed Down into Water

We Bed Down into Water

JOHN RYBICKI

Poems

TRIQUARTERLY BOOKS

NORTHWESTERN UNIVERSITY PRESS

EVANSTON, ILLINOIS

TriQuarterly Books
Northwestern University Press
www.nupress.northwestern.edu

Printed in the United States of America

10 9 8 7 6 5 4 3 2

Library of Congress Cataloging-in-Publication Data

Rybicki, John, 1961–
    We bed down into water : poems / John Rybicki.
       p. cm.
    ISBN-13: 978-0-8101-5187-1 (cloth : alk. paper)
    ISBN-10: 0-8101-5187-1 (cloth : alk. paper)
    ISBN-13: 978-0-8101-5186-4 (pbk. : alk. paper)
    ISBN-10: 0-8101-5186-3 (pbk. : alk. paper)
    I. Title.
    PS3568.Y3977W4 2008
    811.54—dc22
                                        2007035884

For Peter Markus, in the largest sense, brother;

for Martel Epperson—Son, you make my life;

and for my Old World dame who was not born:
she sensed I needed her, slipped down
from some seventeenth-century painting,
and started off across the earth to find me.

≈

Contents

III

Acknowledgments

The author would like to thank the editors at the following magazines, in which these poems first appeared:

Antioch Review: "So Quiet Sending"
Avatar Review: "The Violin Now, My God the Violin"
Blackbird: "The Earth Is Not Quiet"
Bomb: "Sleep Piling Up, Sleep Coming On," "This Sun"
Failbetter: "Julie Ovary Song," "Two Movements for Martel Epperson,"
    "Yellow-Haired Girl with Spider"
Field: "Love Is the Heel That Knocks Hard Against the Floor"
5_Trope: "Fire Psalm"
Gulf Coast: "Fire Psalm Revisited"
The Iowa Review: "Her Body Like a Lantern Next to Me," "Julie Ann
    in the Bone Marrow Unit, Zion, Illinois," "A Song for Kay Mullen"
Michigan Quarterly Review: "The Boy"
New Orleans Review: "Helena's Hair," "Tire Shop Poem"
Nidus: "Outside the Bone Marrow Unit"
North American Review: "Me and My Lass, We Are a Poem,"
    "Not Knowing Enough About Physics to Write This Poem,"
    "Our Romance"
Northwest Review: "Bulrushes," "King"
Poetry: "The Story"
Quarterly West: "Interlochen Center for the Arts"
TriQuarterly: "Say My Name"
Willow Springs: "Thirty Years Ago"

The author would also like to thank the following: Carnegie Mellon University Press for publishing "This Sun" in its anthology *American Poetry: The Next Generation;* June Cotner for publishing "Outside the Bone Marrow Unit" in her collection *Get Well Wishes: Prayers, Poems, and Blessings;* Fairview Press for selecting "Julie Ann in the Bone Marrow Unit, Zion, Illinois" and "Outside the Bone Marrow Unit" for inclusion in *The Cancer Poetry Project;* and Wayne State University Press for including "Interlochen Center for the Arts," "Julie Ann in the Bone Marrow Unit, Zion, Illinois," and "King" in its *New Poems from the Third Coast.*

The author gratefully acknowledges Nancy Eimers, Jack Gilbert, and Philip Levine, whose phrases fortified these poems.

God bless the Carnegie Fund for Authors, the Academy of American Poets, and the Pen American Center for their timely support. When the fiscal wheels fell off our wagon, the following souls were also there to lift us up: Winnie Holzman and Paul Dooley, Karen Parisian, Nina Feirer, Joey Dietz, Denise Duhamel, Norm and Maureen Campbell, and brother Ben and sister Lisa.

Special thanks to John Philip Roberts and Matt Cashen for their astute eyes in the editing of these poems.

Bless the Goebel and Frie clans, in particular Grandpa John—great heart and second father to this boy. Widest thanks to the Delton District and Richland Community Libraries. And as for Stuart Dybek, Amy Hempel, Philip Levine, and Jack Ridl—the other stalwart souls in my corner—I will have to build each of you a rocking chair in the next life.

In memory of John Woods, Ed Mullen, Aunt Jean, Billy Goltz, and Herb Scott—with sufficient reason.

We Bed Down into Water

I

I am feeble and sore broken:
I have roared by reason
of the disquietness of my heart.

—PSALM 38:8

Thirty Years Ago

I lift the night rattler, syringe that will drive my
Julie's stem cell count for the great bone marrow

harvest. 2:15 A.M. and her breasts fall out. My wife
in her near nakedness breathing like a pale bull

through her nose and shaking almost violently.
I fold out the flesh behind the arm, jab her with

the needle whispering, *It's OK. It's OK. Be brave
Dame. Almost done almost done.*

I can feel some breath on my bones flying
me away from my hands until I'm one distant

eye in the future gazing back on this. They boil her
in acid until her hair falls out, lips broil open

with mouth sores. Maybe God's just a skeletal man
sitting on a wooden crate by the river with his face

webbed up in his hands. Earlier today I slipped my hammer
back into its gunslinger slot on the right side of my tool belt,

nabbed a pen from my pocket, and wrote a single word
on the back of my hand. I'm lifting the needle near

Julie's arm when I glance at the word again—already
it is vanishing into the skin below the knuckles.

Barbaric. Then I stab her in the arm
and we climb down our hole into bed.

Julie Ann in the Bone Marrow Unit, Zion, Illinois

Ah Dame, I don't know how else to love you
so I just start juggling. I'm on the street

three floors below your hospital window,
lofting fish or birds that graze against my hands

and fly off, juggling cancer cells and carnations,
slipping in the bowling pin

we snuck out of that alley in Maine. Then I'm juggling
freight trains, and angels, and elephants,

dropping them all. I don't care. So long as you
can stand near your high window and laugh,

so long as you stand near your hospital bed
clapping your hands.

Me and My Lass, We Are a Poem

We tangle our hair in the moon,
then she coughs and I have no net

to catch the cough so I make her hot tea
with honey. I call her my coughing alarm clock,

but she's warmer and smoother than our oven
for waltzing with.

When we travel in our covered wagon,
she's in the bathtub splashing her way

across the prairie, singing Bo Diddley songs.
Any drops she spills

the prairie dogs lick them up.
That's the kind of poem she is.

When we lie down in the earth,
we'll need coffins with holes bored

through their sides: we'll each have
one arm hanging out

so I can take hold of her
hand, even while we're in the dirt.

Some nights our bed floats through
the bedroom wall. We're on our bellies

laughing and rowing with one arm.
When we get tired, the stars

make nice pillows for our heads.
The wind is what wakes me,

blowing so hard I watch my love's skin
flake off: a whole storm of her

flutters away from me until all that's left
inside her is a tired old woman

holding her spine like a candle.

Love Is the Heel That Knocks Hard Against the Floor

I was raw with visions this
day of a God with no skin,
so I held my cup out
our kitchen window
and listened to it rain.

I'd get revisited by the terror
in the silence of a room
without her in it. Logic slips,
panics the rational mind
which whispers back,

you just heard her pony
her heels across the kitchen floor
fifteen seconds ago. Where's she going?
But so many cities have burned
since then, you rush,

you fullback from room to room
crying into an empty house.
"Dude? O Dude?" she says at last,
and you kiss the sound on the mouth
before it washes away.

Tire Shop Poem

What we're all doing is dancing,
gliding under the undercarriage

of this car, our hands trenched
with oil and winter slop that stings

down the neckline of my shirt,
teeth in my pocket because

it's Christmastime and there
are Fannie May chocolates

on the front counter. Try and stop
the flesh and it wiggles out

from inside your gloves and
smashes itself against hubcaps

and rubber—Cooper Cobras
and Tiger Paws—those snare

drumskins we slap, tire after
tire just to listen to something

solid ringing back. I catch this
Adam upstart go red-hot,

beat the clang of pry bar to rim,
swivel the deck and hiss

of air he might with his own
breath be, lips to each valve stem,

blowing these tires up
so he can lie down at night with so many

people riding on his breath over snow,
riding on his breath over leaves.

I catch his dare and rubber roll
a tire up my calf and pop

the center cap, clamp and spin,
hammer lead weights onto rim

after dizzying rim. I lug nut smash
and flick the pry bar from one hand

to the next. Fred Astaire in a
tire shop, where we slap our boots

across all that slop to outdistance
fire, outdistance that burning bush

that follows us everywhere.

A Song for Kay Mullen

For Ed Mullen: 1960–1994

The flaming balls float when our hands
    are busy elsewhere.
Juggling's easy: first, study hypnosis
    and rock your finger
metronome in front of a cross
    on the highway. Go back
to that day when one alphabet devoured
    another. You have two animals
with their brights on, their eyes following
    the ticktock rock of your finger,
so the cross with the dusty flowers
    around its neck evaporates
under a mother's pillow.
    If you've done your job right,
the locomotive lofts over her boy's truck,
    all squeal and shiver and brace.
He's on his way to work, 6:30 A.M.:
    an airport needs to be built
and his body is burning to build it.
    That night the mother wakes
to the creak of her son's hooves in the hall
    when the boy gets up to pee,
and the sound of that gush is enough
    to roll a mother over safe,

the red dial under her lungs spinning
    this way and that,
where a husband sometimes reaches
    to undress her and give thanks,
chandelier his skin upon her.
    The tumblers under the red dial
click into place as the boy pees
    and the mother listens
to the comforting steam of her children
    breathing in those rooms
that box out around her and become her
    larger body. Her heart spins
like the fiery wheel on her boy's pickup
    after it flips a half dozen times
but not tonight, not with you on the roadside
    rocking your finger hypnotic
at the oncoming engine. In the closet,
    even the feathers in the boy's coat
flutter a little then settle as he flushes
    and the floorboards creak
with what keeps a mother's back
    from breaking, the round piano
notes of a boy walking towards
    his bedroom to sleep.

The Earth Is Not Quiet

Even leaves are rattling
out of hearts. I gravel skid
and dive over my handlebars.
I know what the leaves are:

one formed from the heart of
the priest lifting this skinny boy
like some host five feet off
the altar and hanging him

from the pins in Christ's feet;
one shaped from the heart of
the German man on the line at
Dodge Truck, seventy-one years

old and he's still stretching
Cinderella's slipper
over 487 brake pedals each day,
fire and floating metal carriages

and sweat blown back around him
as if gathering in a twirling midnight
dress; another leaf for the nurse
her fingers hollow as bone flutes

and she's piping them all night
beside her boy's oxygen tent;
another leaf for the father, who,
three hours earlier, slammed the rolling

hospital bed through doctors to find
a wall socket that would give
his blue boy oxygen. The boy
diving over his handlebars

because maybe this time the leaf
is the father's heart falling.

Our Romance

I'm beside my father at a red light on Alter and Kercheval as a boy, my
booze-lamp pops saying, "You couldn't kill someone if you had to," to a
son axed in half by tenderness. Pops, who bare-knuckle brawls with his
grown boy to punch breathing holes through his armor and love me
through them; who welts my arms and jaw with blows as I do my Sugar
Ray duck and weave and spring in under his oak fists, cup my hand
around his cheek, and stop everything. See, he's trying to hold his son,
hold his son with blows. He snaps a straight jab, whips a right, then
left hook. It looks like he's trying to wrap his boy tenderly up, if you could
only see it in slow motion. Pops, who half headlocks his son after, laughing
as if someone is using a rough knife to carve the sounds out of him.

"I'd kick your ass in a fight," he says. "You know why?"

"Why? I wanna know why."

"Because you won't hit your old man, but your old man will
hit you."

Pops, who has a knife-wound slash like a strap from his shoulder to
his opposite hip, who gave up drinking to throw iron and swim laps. He
flexes his gladiator chest in our living room, his boys on either side cup-
ping their hands around his rock biceps, tracing their hands along his
sloping lats. Pops, who used to hand me his coat when he got home then
sucker punch me in the gut. "We're going into the yard. I've got to kick
your ass before you get any bigger. Patsy, I'm taking Johnny into the
yard to kick his ass"—laughing, throwing his arm around my neck—
"only you better watch out, I fight dirty."

Pops, whose ma died when he was six months old; who danced on barroom tables to get money to go to Saint Joe's; danced until his dad's cigarette-toothed friends sprinkled coins at his feet. Until one day in the alley, near the kitchen door, old lady Bernardini shouted back into the bar, "Frances, it's that Rybicki boy, here to beg again."

I'm back home and he's loving me. I mean, really loving me. Staggering from the garage to the kitchen with his arm around my neck, when he turns like a man on a wedding cake and slaps me in the face.

"Slap me back again," he says, his light blue eyes beaming, *it's so good to see my boy.*

We're face-to-face. I can't hit what I love. He smacks me again, not too hard, but hard enough. I slap him back.

"Come on, harder," he says and whacks me one full in the face, something like tenderness breaking open in him.

"Come on," Pops says. "I want to feel alive."

This Tape Measure Made of Light

1

We have some say in this skin we wear,
    the movie screen we paint over it.
We will it in public to be so-and-so,
    but there are red lights that halt
the steaming herd. We thank God for our hole,
    our hiding place, the hound
smacking its tail when we arrive, a kite
    ripping dumbly down our driveway.

2

At a job site, snapped off from the familiar,
    we're lowering trusses onto a flat roof
then tying them together. There's a seven-
    story grain elevator spraying dust,
and what with the rain and the fermentation,
    we have a dairy farm on the roof,
a real shit storm to slop around in.
    We bang like this, our hammers
and our blood, to test along these verges,
    to hear something solid ringing back.
There's the hopper below us hissing
    and pouring nutritious pellets
for dogs and horses, pouring gravity-
    fed into the big sacks. We climb

down the chute through this hole like a navel.
　　Two men down there with earmuffs on,
and they're tossing the sacks onto a dolly all day.
　　The young one senses animal
movement, my flicking a brushstroke
　　of blood on him.
He looks up at me and nods
　　and I nod back. It's an old light
that passes between us, and I make it
　　into a nice rope, and I hold on.

　　3
Take a pinch of light from under the rib.
　　Let's see how far it stretches:
this filament to measure your rafters
　　to their tails, Lord.
How will you frame, say, a window
　　in this house so a Milky Way
spills through it? Only so many fingers
　　pinch at these fissures,
these light beams through
　　every pore, every knothole.
What we long for or have lost
　　lurks under those floorboards
we nail down knowing they're not floorboards.
　　Our molecules rain outward,
which means we're always leaving
　　someone. And our tired selves
line up behind us
　　like men looking for work.

Outside the Bone Marrow Unit

It has been over a year since Julie waved
aside the wheelchair and walked in her own bright bones

out of that sterilized chamber: the butterfly
doors swung open and she walked out into air

that two weeks earlier could have killed her.
I'm worried that writing about cancer,

thinking about cancer, will start cancer
growing again inside her. Where in that sweet void,

where in those wide heavens
could it be hiding?

I stand on my toes and kiss one of my angels,
and in that kiss beg her

to take a stiff broom to this talk:
sweep the cancer back across the heavens;

please don't miss one crumb of it. Sweep
the cancer back into its black box of oblivion.

II

There is a song, bird song or wind song,
or the song old rooms sing when no one
is awake to hear. For a moment I
almost catch the melody we make
with bare walls, old iron sagging beds
and scarred floors. There is one
deep full note for each of us.
This is the first night of my life
I know we are music.

—PHILIP LEVINE

Interlochen Center for the Arts

I'm tired of being locked up, living inside a high C note, bedding down in a soprano voice that never draws breath. Tonight my legs took root in a liquid earth: I tried floating out to sea until I was dead: I wanted to know whom I'd travel back to and love one last time before I drowned. Every morning pianos float past my cabin window like lazy barges. Children dive in and find harps hidden in piles of thorns and then these kids line up beside four maples and start dragging their bows across each trunk as if sawing them down—as if each tree were a string on a giant cello they were born to play to perfection.

I walk around all day punching one pointed toe into the earth in front of me to make sure it's still there. It's like someone tore a piece of cloth off Christ's coat and we're all floating around on it. I'm up there, up here, and by the third week I've stopped using "like" or "as." I'm ninety percent sure I'm dead and that's heaven tuning up out there.

There's a terror to this world. I'm afraid to see anyone I know: Ma, Pa, Joey, Leo. . . . I'm terrified I dreamed their voices, dreamed the people around me: highway tides of drivers sputtering to life when I approach; men and women with jackhammer drills, library cards, butcher knives; terrified I have arms and hands I can't see, arms and hands I slip into their bodies when I get close, and with one hand around the back of each heart like a baby's head, start pumping them back to life, so I'll have someone in the world to talk to.

The Violin Now, My God the Violin

Lord, you nail your angels down
in such a fleshy house.

We're all hides and heads
mounted in a sky

that scrolls itself away from us.
We just want to lie down

in our own blood
at night and float.

≈

Days we find the violin
washed up: we try it and it floats.

It makes a fine house.
We remember the strings that stretched

from our mother's navel
to her throat.

The way we'd pluck them
with a broom handle

over our heads
dusting for cobwebs.

≈

The tablecloths are so white
and pretty here

when we're not scraping
skyscrapers off our plates.

Now our bodies live
in the water. We try to remember

the rowing out of her
that produced this ache.

In the cafeteria, we dip
our spoons into our bowls

of soup. It's dusty
at the bottom if, say,

you carve a violin
out of a woman's hand.

≈

You sow the soil
in the musty hull of our boat.

Some prefer cherry trees
in their violins for climbing.

Nights at the football games
are lovely too: you trample the stands

with the rest of the herd,
swallow the halogen lights.

You are powerful.
You have a violin at home and it floats.

Strange fish thump
against your walls: proof

that a mother's heart goes on
knocking.

≈

Of course, your violin leaks
when it rains. The rain taps all night

into your coffee cups,
your chamber pots. You feel like drowning

each night, don't you?
You line your walls with socks,

and your arms fall like vines
all over the floor.

Fire Psalm

Alexander the Great, Genghis Khan,
and all the little unknown assassins

who dunk their mouths into holy water
drunk and bobbing at the bottom for—

you know what—baby's heads
not apples. I know a tree askew,

where children dangle by those o
so slender umbilical cords feeding

light into their heads. God if I were
only just blood, an animal governed

by appetite and piss—I'd go back
to my hands around my own neck,

legs like broken timepieces dangling
below that stem. I know a tree

where you can snap a child off
by his head and bite into his skin

and lift the shiny side after, lift it
way up over your head:

Here you go, God, you light
junkie, bite into this.

Bulrushes

My wife and I in the dark
    and she's kissing
my palm. I ease it around
    the tumors in the back
of her neck—fat tulip bulbs—
    and cradle her down.

Tomorrow I will lay my hand
    against our blacktop street,
turn it into river. A child
    in a basket will come floating,
and I will rush out
    midstream to get her.

Two Movements for Martel Epperson

From a letter to Marie Howe

Dearest Marie,

    There's this rope around my son's waist,
city he's towing like some glacier
      across our cornfield. Forget my romance

    with bricks stacked like loaves of bread.
We have little Detroit castles
      crumbling all over our field.

    That city of stone where blackbirds
buzz in and out of windows
      blown open by rocks.

    Martel is emptying his pockets.
There's a man in an orange vest tonight
      wandering among those piles.

    He's following a blood trail through
the scruff of prairie grass.
      Just a few weeks ago Julie dreamed

    our son held his BB gun
to her head
      and pulled the trigger.

I was his Big Brother last summer
riding the roller coasters then dropping him off
      at his own little castle.

It floats so close to our house
the front doors are kissing. Glass shatter
      on his porch someone had swept

into a sparkling pile. We were chins up
to the brick-sized window on his front door
      crying into an empty house for his mom:

"Annie? Annie, you in there?" My brother
Benny out of his cherry SUV and we gather ourselves
      around this boy and what to do.

We're two loaves of white bread
on Martel's porch and I'm scribbling a note to his mom.
      "I'm so sorry, Mr. Rybicki," Martel says,

tears in a landslide down his cheeks.
Days later, when we key into her house,
      Martel crosses the hardwood floor

to the bullet holes.
The walls seem so fleshy and tall.
      He slips his fingers in

the holes and leaves them there.
He's at the bottom of a climbing wall
      wanting to scale his way up the sky.

And so this hawk of a boy lights in our nest.
I don't know how to hug him right.
   There's something sharp like a city

   in between us. So I warm his blanket
in the dryer and cover him sleeping on the sofa.
   He moves in and on the third day

   his lungs go bad—he's a wheezer like I am.
I pour medicine from a vial and breathe with him
   when he hookahs mist into his lungs.

   When he comes out of sleep, he flashes
his face at me, an oil spill made of boy light.
   "Hey Scooty Puff Daddy Senior," he says.

   "Hey Venison Meatball Rex," I call back.
What we say every syllable after that is for the first time.
   Martel and I do *Speed Racer* mornings,

   my coffee all rock-a-bye up our driveway
as he snatches off the dashboard a sliding plate
   of toast. We're off to school

   in the dark with that hawk of light in the east.
At night he races marbles along the sloping counter,
   the marbles doing wind sprints. "They're football players,"

   he says and lets them roll and bump heads.
Then he's whispering, "Go-go-go fire defense,"
   playing coach to a bunch of marbles.

I'm fire in the woodstove and stir the pot,
and out of nowhere this boy who once swallowed gasoline
on a dare is dangling his Fancy hamster Ginger

so her back paws light on his little skateboard.
I'm talking rubber band wars where cowboys
dive for cover, bullets whizzing past

our bookshelves, or taking off an ear.
So many miracles our roof's no more
than the lid to a baby grand tilted up

so the singing can ring and rafter up.
"You're living two lives now," I tell him rolling out
of Detroit in my truck with glass tabletops,

sofas, plastic fruit (his mom is being evicted).
"You slip your arms out of a fur coat made of bricks.
And when we get home, trade it

for a fur coat made of cornfields."
He smiles one deep breath and says,
"I like the fur coat made of corn the best."

≈

Dearest Marie,

Your letter brought music to our branches
after so hard a day here. Today Martel smacked
in the head a little boy named Hunter.

Tonight we gathered in the field with his teachers,
principal, basketball coach and lay hands on
    his old house, that whale thrown up on our land.

And when the good boy gets tired
and drains out of him, we haul our son to Lake Michigan.
    He's such a beautiful kite

    smacking up and down the dunes.
The light on the water and sand he loots
    into his pockets and shoes.

At home he paints on his bedroom wall
freighters and beach fires and waves
    that spray out at you.

In the foreground, there's a black dot
of a boy with a white mom and dad.
    The boy's flying up the wall holding our hands.

The sand Martel brought back
he piles on his bedsheets, shaping it into castles
    and hills.

I have seen him bow to his snare drum
and place his mouth inside it
    like he's drinking from a birdbath

    or shimmering pool—the drumskin vibrating
so its molecules flow in and out.
    He hawks his wings over the drumhead,

but Julie and I are gone. We're out in the field
tearing bread from the cornerstone of some old house,
gathering warm bits for under his pillow.

Yellow-Haired Girl with Spider

Once a spider lived under her arm and
so she never shaved. She let her hair
grow gnarl for that spider to nest in.
She'd slipper step the wet grass night
with her wet grass feet and hold a bare
lightbulb up under her hairy arm
with the hairy spider living inside it.
She'd keep that one arm raised until
fat moths and June bugs and beetles
and swarms of mosquitoes tangled in her
armpit, trembling and pinned down,
exhausting themselves until the spider
slipped from warm cave top
to sting those moths and beetle
bugs and June bugs and mosquitoes,
sting them over and over with that
one kiss I could not live without.

Say My Name

Say my name is *ash* and I keep it in my pocket to play with. Say I'm hammering my fingers on the air like there's a piano floating there always in front of me, minstrel from town to town searching for now who? Now *who's* a good sound to try through your fingers, owl-like, like *who who*, only I wish my fingers were little trumpets, no, little guitars with amplifiers stacked so I could do my best Santana and sound through a certain city these amplifications—a kind of war cry for the tender. I'd announce my coming forth with that squall like some zany ship with its hull splitting through the concrete, parting the dying elms and slapping paperboys off their bikes: that ocean liner gliding along the blacktop, plowing the earth to a halt outside her house so she'd have to look up and telescope even to see who it was waving to her from the deck of that ship.

Her Body Like a Lantern Next to Me

There's this movie I am watching:
my love's belly almost five months
    pregnant with cancer,

    more like a little rock wall
piled and fitted inside her
    than some prenatal rounding.

Over there's her face
near the frying pan she's bent over,
    but there's no water in the pan,

and so, no reflection. No pool
where I might gather such a thing as a face,
    or sew it there on a tablet made of water.

To have and to haul it away,
sometimes dipping into her
    in the next room that waits for me.

    ≈

I am old at this. I am stretching
the wick again into my throat
    when the flame burns down.

She's splashing in the tub
and singing, *I love him very much,*
    though I'm old and tired

    and cancerous. It's spring
and now she's stopping traffic,
    lifting one of her painted turtles

    across the road. Someone's honking,
pumping an arm out the window,
    cheering her on.

    She falls then like there's a house
on her back, hides her head in the bank grass
    and vomits into the ditch.

    ≈

    She keeps her radioactive linen,
bowl, and spoon separate. For seven days
    we sleep in different rooms.

    Over there's the toilet she's been
heaving her roots into. One time I heard her
    through the door make a toast to it,

    Here's to you, toilet bowl.
There's nothing poetic about this.
    I have one oar that hangs

    from our bedroom window,
and I am rowing our hut
    in the same desperate circle.

≈

I warm her tea then spread
cream cheese over her bagel,
    and we lie together like two guitars,

    a rose like a screw
in each of our mouths.
    There's that liquid river of story

that sometimes sweeps us away
    from all this, into the ha ha
and the tender. At night the streetlights

    buzz on again with the stars,
and the horses in the field swat their tails
    like we will go on forever.

    ≈

    I'm at my desk herding some
lost language when I notice how quiet
    she has been. Twice I call her name

    and wait after my voice has lost its legs
and she does not ring back.
    Dude, I'm still here, she says at last,

    then the sound of her
stretching her branches, and from them
    the rain falling thick through our house.

I'm racing to place pots and pans
everywhere. Bottle her in super canning jars.
For seventeen years, I've lined

the shelves of our root cellar with them.
One drop for each jar.
I'll need them for later.

Helena's Hair

I have a switchblade Christ
can't even feel. I carve one drop

out of his eye
and he's one drop lighter.

Julie says, "You and Pete
are anarchists; you get the same spark
out of breaking rules."

I night climbed your elm once,
until the trunk split,

and I had one foot on either side
of the wish.

The branches became wooden ropes,
then bicycle chains,
then Helena's hair:

her bright hand in a window
is opening and closing,

as the houses welded to this world
gallop in a circle around her.

Not Knowing Enough About Physics to Write This Poem

> Even our skeletons are in love.
> —JULIE MOULDS

I want our ashes in the same jar, our energy
    fields like a sparking night,
or a day dumbfounded by bees.

We're in a field of sunflowers, our atoms
    suffuse and particulate,
buzzing away at this willow out there.

His hair's pouring around the face
    of the other willow he's dancing with.
He's dipping her under that waterfall

of green and shivering time,
    in time to my love's breathing.
We hear him pom-pom outside our window

at night, his roots snapping the sidewalk.
    Julie and I rush to
the window and pose.

I dip her with the candle on the table
    behind us, candle that lights
our silhouettes for passersby.

≈

I'm twirling her skirt just above the mud,
    replicating in selves so
frenzied with her

atomized in my arms.
    I am galloping away from her,
portioning out this abundance,

tossing torches onto straw roofs,
    waking those people who've
been waiting their whole lives

to stand in the street in their slippers,
    loop their arms around
each other and watch their lives burn.

    ≈

One finger immersed in the iron pot,
    I boil water, or lay a flaked-
off piece of Julie's skin

on a dying woman's tongue—a sizzling
    of particles in itself. In the dark,
my love's rapturous wails

turn to whispers, a hummingbird hovering
    still near my ear.
My horse lunges away over logs

and mucks down drumbeats, splashing a kind
    of just-being-born music. Someday I'll be
that monk transcribing the music

we make when we beat our palms, beat our hooves
    against this muddy drum;
the monk dipping one feather in a bowl

to stain the sky with half and quarter note coals,
    to stain that sky that's always
scrolling itself away from us

with our music branded to its hide.
    This so we can replicate the music
we made with our *long and glorious dying.*

    ≈

By night we sit in the vast music
    parlors with our ancestors.
We're piecing together our own mastodons,

our bodies large and dependent for a while
    on heart and lung and nail.
We sit beside our ancestors replaying

the melody we make with bare walls, *old iron*
    sagging beds, and scarred floors.
My love and I hide in a pool

of lamplight, then I gallop
    off on horseback along her compass,
the red hooves drumming over her

land and skin, and beneath
    where her heart is stamping its foot.
I want to give away our excess,

to sing with hammer smacking wood,
    sing with hands
that brand that blue sky

rubbing its hide against mine.
    To open my mouth and sing,
returning God to God.

    ≈

I gaze upon her blue water and sky, her wedding
    dress replete with phlox
and bees. Forgive me if I'm amazed

when my love's fingers close around mine
    and sting. To be certain,
her hand in mine—that miracle, sensation—

can swirl a field of sunflowers down a willow's trunk
    to its muddy feet. How could anyone live
without their season of touching?

    ≈

The man with white coat, and of course,
    black-rimmed glasses,
checks with a clown's lipstick

an *x* next to sensation, stands there
    impervious to those blackbirds
I'll get to in a minute, the black minutiae

of my love's fingers in the valley of bones
    beneath my button-down shirt.
She's lifting and tearing as I'm

fluttering back to where skirts billow
    and float a woman up
without a man given liberties of seeing anything,

though I knew that first day, above her lavender
    anklet stockings—that tease
of flesh I devoured from across the room—

knew sweeter what I could not see,
    under that umbrella of fabric
higher and higher, was a muscle,

a molecular thread laced everywhere
    through flesh to make a madness
out of touching.

        ≈

Sometimes I leave my lips on her
    belly in one spot for days,
because I'm terrified the ways

she might vanish, flesh like some trick hankie
    yanked suddenly into heaven.
We chain the dogs

outside, our buttons flinging themselves
    against the wall. I take her breast
in my mouth and bite her hard,

cup the other, then tender her neck
    down to our bed the way some
men set a bottle of fine wine on a napkin

or lower an infant to the cradle. Outside our dogs
    bite each other's ears
and nuzzle necks as our cries rise

through the body along the rafter strings,
    tremor through the spider's knitting
until those boats rock back to harbor,

rock back to that stillness, and we bed down
    into water,
bed down into night.

    ≈

I try and live a hound's serene life,
    sip my milk and roll so
my paws kick against that underbelly of sky,

vast in its waves that frenzy about
    our skulls. Now we're at
an ice-cream parlor

near the window. This right now
    I can count on: the shiver
of the cone, her red lips,

the heat from her cheekbones
    on the back of my hand.
There are days I leave yogurt cups

at job sites to prove the next day
    I was really there. There's a terror
when her car's not in the driveway,

a rip that won't seal itself up. She has vanished
    through that hole
in the air. Her shimmer has

drenched the hickory bark and grass
    and pole barn metal—that definitive skin
we hammered into place.

There in the ice-cream parlor,
    there in the shivering liquid stillness
the impossible happens: she wipes her mouth

with the back of her hand and it hisses
    as it travels to her shining teeth.
She laughs and out gusts such flames,

and the birds peck away in the ditches
    coughing up
the beginning of the world.

Long Before This Tenderness Between Us Was Born

Whitman knew he was a drop
of light that fell splashing against
the mud and landed upright a man

sprouting calves and hips, the sweet
fruit already ringing in his chest.
Imagine the orchestra of drops

pouring from God's face, long before
the throat became a smokestack,
long before this tenderness between us

was born, there was a mouth rising
from the ground to pool like some
birdbath under you, a drum

where your navel sits, and a hut
whose walls were bathed in lamplight.
Tonight you listen to our daughter sleep.

You flick her bedroom light off
because it's the one hard star
you are in charge of.

You lean in the doorway
pouring your blood
up to our daughter's throat

where it sits like some blanket
you keep even though she lives
on the outside of you now.

So Quiet Sending

Not elephants in a train
to your door,

not sunflowers that bloom
through the concrete

so your old Impala
has to swerve.

I have no need for air,
nor any fruit,

no need for bite
a chip from the moon.

I want to send so quiet,
so quiet as a barn

spreading its arms
to sing to you.

Could I tap out
only your initials?

Would you hear
the white space roar

around them? I want to
send so quiet,

this house that
feels like prayer.

Snow

Sweet dirt, sweet grass
my tongue is hot

for your skin
is not spoken around here.

These chains are
snow cuff links

slicing open
our rib cages.

We oppose this.
Your skin, my skin

it hives against the air.
Isn't that delicious

to be heaven floating
around in a sack of skin?

The alphabet has how many trillion
new characters since

man was born?
Who is dying?

Who is dying to form?
What slot do we shove

the diamonds in?
My lips cannot bear this.

I must breathe
with my mouth

a holy o locked
open forever.

Fire Psalm Revisited

Lord, tilt your lamps
so the oil flows up

out of man. Take away
this relentless burning.

Let the stars sip
on my fires like tea.

Take the scalding light
back into heaven,

where bodies are built
for such things.

III

Julie Ovary Song

> She's gone. She was my love, my moon or more.
> She chased the chickens out and swept the floor.
> —JAMES WRIGHT

The sandhill cranes carroo and shadow over
high chair and crib, the baby's room
a giddy shivering blue. The bolt

that bores a hole through the center slips down
the throat. I rear from the ground with this
burned down tenement for a hat, I wear

bruise circles around my love's eyes. Sundown,
this flaming beard on the water pulls itself
away from us while my wife's hand

reaches to tug it closer. Cool Lake Daddy,
are these waters your kiss? Are tumors bells
and will our bones rot like so many roots?

The balloon of her lungs blows, and she floats away
without me. My mouth sounds rusty when I say,
I'm leaving for work.

My little saltshaker rattles in the dark.
One deep kiss by the door, then she flickers
our porch light dizzy, her light on

the outside of the flesh. I windmill my window down,
my lips out in the cool as her cry
washes the hill:

I love you Dude. Be careful Dude.

≈

Listen to my bird in the bathtub splashing
and singing old sitcom tunes. It's the *M*A*S*H*
theme song tonight.

I scratch the door and open it a crack,
see those brown eyes through the steam,
the way her head nods its surrender

to one side. Morning walks where
the wind hits my scarecrow on a stick,
straw flying everywhere from her sleeve

and from her neck where I knot a scarf
tight to lock it in. See her mitten waving,
Bye-bye my Johnny,

when I follow her out in my socks, the ashy
autumn way she rises above our hill,
something like sawdust

blown off her layers. She's disintegrating,
flaking down to elemental, no blood boot
solid to moor her to this world.

Why not just say my love may be dying?
Because I want you to drown with me.

Sleep Piling Up, Sleep Coming On

Even the foxhound bellies down in mud,
    his locomotive tongue, his regal stance
as blackbirds gather into one swooping bird.

Death's like that, a sodden blanket
    too heavy for the line in my yard.
I am an owl, eyes, all eyes,

spooked into motion by the red hammer
    hammering red pegs, the sky itself,
a red hawk that glides across the tongue

but will not light. From my perch, the oaks,
    the maples with their giddy schoolboy
shiverings, their stranglehold on light.

The upward way they churn their oars in fire:
    together now, row boys, row.
The creak and pitch of this ship,

houses along a deck that rocks then rights
    itself, the red fruit blazing
in their windows at night. I'm underneath

this canopy, this hickory with its roots
    that break the concrete, crack it
into charts and maps I cannot read.

Pin me to this floating wall, the foxhound
    like some fleshy anchor,
the canvas flapping this way and that,

and in my great unknowing what signs
    are these and how do I name them:
the hawk through my mouth, the featherless

houses, a hand like a branch shadow in an
    open window, the sky blown about
and parted with light and dark.

The Story

Someone floats through your middle
with a spine like a candle, a nightgown
over it and you see through the simple talk,

the blood bell gone again like fading action,
the slug you moment in a story, then after
when the body hums warm and electric

with what it can't hold on to. Let's say
the very action of living—heart and lungs—
is a printing press of selves.

If you are lucky, flashing, maybe millions
of the selves who loved the girl coalesce,
recline at night, and lie down in her circle,

your circle still opening for her. Some
nights you blink to find her mouth biting
through the same pear,

that sweet opening, that new flavored kiss.
If you are lucky, you press on with the same
wobbly shopping cart the two of you

pushed out of Egypt or ancient Rome,
pushed out of sparking glaciers when the body
first filled with such a frightening thunder.

And when the curtain darkens to blood,
the old wooden porches with their swings
rock as if the wind were kicking its legs.

Are you aware? Each day one more hankie
gets tugged up from the blood house,
and you are one day less in this hard Eden.

This Sun

I train into this city of mud and brick and collide
with my sis, her friends clanging around me,

the city itself smeared in Rybicki rouge—all those bricks
humming their energy fields inside each mason's palm.

God how this city necks my neck with its fur coat of bricks;
those red-hot dawns I dip my bushel basket

into heaven's own fire and drench it down over rooftops
and power lines and steaming beds; pouring that fire

across the grass and concrete grids of streets.
I flick my fingers over the flaming beds,

lift in one palm what we call sun, tow it in
my oxen's cart slowly out over the world, my hand

to my own mouth blowing kisses back
at all those hearts exploding in my nest.

King

James's husky King disappears under one tiny square of snow in the ghetto. We're in our T-shirts yelling "King! King!" off the porch and there's nothing but white powder out there, white tundra, the heart's wildness. We're shouting "Here, King!" from the porch where nights before we cracked off rounds from James's revolvers, "You gotta let 'em know what you got or they'll come get some." On the porch in just our T-shirts yelling to the hound over such sweet desolation—electric lines, cinder block walls, monkey bars thick-boned with snow—we don't see him. The white kettle of his breath steams up, the hound bounding suddenly out of white powder and pounding towards us with these iceberg hunks of snow spilling off his coat. And Christ, if that wasn't wild enough, all those cinder block walls, I-beam and brick miles ignite, turn to white ash, like it's God's breath reforging an iron cake. The Belle Isle and Ambassador bridges pull down suddenly in a gust; the hound hauling himself out of deep powder in arch after arch, every drop of light and heart and energy burning forward through his muscles, burning out through his eyes and trained on us. Every river of concrete, every fuming car, every power line is just bad music, a mistake he can fix by letting snow settle over him, then thundering out of the earth come morning.

Saint Clare of Montefalco

Sister Corrin had been warned not to let the flame-haired boy into her choir. I had a tie up tight against my throat and this glass-cracking voice. Man, I wanted to sing. Mrs. Kellet kept warning that slender nun off. I sat in front by choice after that, something a mischief-sniffing kid like me would never have done. I sat in front in music class and blasted that soprano right into the gut of my bad rep. Sister Corrin could not sit still in her white fatigues, could not bear to hear this sweet bird out there and not throw her white shawl around him, not add his voice to the heavenly liftoff that went on behind the altar on Sundays. After six weeks of this, Sister Corrin could bear no more, and kept me in after class. I vowed. She smiled. This was the fourth grade. I lasted five glorious weeks before I got the boot, before I reclaimed my seat mixed up with the other bad boys in the back of that room. But I want you to know, there was a time when I floated out over the front of the altar in my altar boy smock, and I've been a sinner ever since.

Silhouette

I'm folding clothes when
I notice my boy lying curled
on our street in the rain,

lying there with his hood up.
No cars, just the rain
with its soft bites.

I'm in a rush outside
when Martel begins to
rise, careful-like,

and when he's all the way up,
he stares at the dry outline
of his body on the blacktop,

his face bowed like he's
reading something.
His friend Chucky comes

trolling on his bike, skidding
his sneakers on the street.
Martel lifts his chin

and then both boys look
down again, watching
my son disintegrate.

The Boy

We're all of us shrapnel flung from the same barrel.
Remember, God's passed out after six days of mainlining light.
We carry his awful weather like the memory of fire,

our bones shaped to huddle around such a flame.
We wait a long time to chisel a little of it into a woman,
shooting blind where the stone in her waters

gives in to our scrawl . . . *so lovers can dwell at last
in a single body.* What we call a rib cage is only a mother
and father's hands cupped around a child's red breath.

Our son cracks heads on a football field, fists the heavy
bag in our barn, races me doing sit-ups and push-ups—
this to harden the bread before bedtime.

He's that black lightbulb snowboarding at Timber Ridge.
He leaps to ride the rail he's seen on TV, but cracks
one of his branches in the fall.

I don't mind raking leaves, or breaking rubber off of rims
for him, cracking one sharp stone against a page until it sheds
the proper sparks. I'm in my truck rumbling home

from the tire shop when this herd of music
goes shredding through the corn, and it's keeping pace
    with my pickup. I'm tapping the dashboard in time

    when a barn appears way out there caving in on a field,
its boards shaped like piano keys I might pluck
    if only God gave me such a reach.

We must be two houses. There's that room that widens
inside us under the skylights God left in our heads. Five times
    the cancer has rung its bells in my love's body.

    Five times we have stuffed them with cotton.
So no fleshy miracle for us (wife, forgive me) no baby
    popping between my love's legs.

We hover as one starling over this boy we've been given.
He's sleeping belly down tonight with one arm
    hanging overboard and he's rowing,

he's pawing at those waters that once rocked him.
One stroke and his bed goes through our walls—inordinate power—
    another stroke and it glides a full city block.

So many streetlights slip past his glass-bottom boat,
those luminescent bobbers he might take into his mouth.
    Now he's trolling around his blood mom's house—

    there's no wake for the fish to feed on, but he's circling
to see through the window where his mom is sleeping
    on a sofa, or throwing up into a bowl.

There he goes watching himself go room to room
hiding hunks of food in his pockets for later—bits of Honey Buns,
    or oatmeal cookies with the icing in the middle

    you can get for a quarter. And there go her bottles—
wine coolers, half-pints, forty-ounce jumbos—
    bobbing around his boat. Tonight he raps on

    our bedroom door, tells us he has to make himself thin
after taking all this food into his mouth: Soft 'n' Good white bread,
    cheeseburgers, and strawberries, Concord grapes in season.

Each time he sleeps, the prayer book closes,
one more page across the side of his face.
    We are older up our ladder, my love and I.

Over there's the coffeepot with its black honey
that'll run down the vine come morning, that apple or hare
    that keeps our blood going on its course

    towards that tombstone we'll one day hug to our chest
like a favorite book. Stranger. Charcoal. Son.
    I have made this fist inside my chest for you.

Let us pretend together for awhile,
whitewash these walls, build a house within a house.
    Ignore how the trees outside work their arms

    like a drowning man. When you tinker with an old engine
in the barn, or find our hound lost in a blizzard
    and he licks your neck all the way home,

I haul away your sparks in our wheelbarrow
and pile them all day in our yard. We must be two houses,
     the body and the spirit. Let us be actors with one of them.

Tonight you made a snowmobile out of a clothespin,
and one of those giant black-clamp paper clips. You took the springs
     from two of my pens to give your rider legs:

he's scooting the white tundra on my writing desk.
I can hear you wheezing on the other side of this wall of books.
     I stop and lean my little weight upon it,

     push the wall down over you like warm bread.
Son, I know the grass is green fire waiting for our mouths.
     Hush now, hush.

Three Lanterns

There's our son at the end of my hook
    riding over the Detroit River

where Tecumseh's still rowing
    towards his oblivion.

This boy we're casting to the land
    of the leaping frogs.

My lass lives on the floor
    where the fish are frying,

her spine snapped in half
    the way a Milky Way might.

She squares her thumbs and fingers together,
    frames for our son

a picture window to climb through.

    ≈

Eighteen months with us
    and our dark-skinned son

still has pockets sewn over his clothes.
    They're filled with stones

that keep a boy underwater,
    his vowels bubbling up to us.

With our brooms and hockey sticks,
    we're swatting away

city streetlights that followed him here,
    those bulbs that bow

and peck at his back.

    ≈

My love's trying to stop the chiming,
    her fingers so singular

since that one dark bell of cancer
    is ringing again in her neck.

I hollow this house while she sleeps,
    take my time and chisel

the proper curve so our canoe
    cuts easy through rough water.

My lass is a sweet tomahawk
    for the scalping

of moons and runaway boys.

    ≈

We hold hands over our son's
    mouth when he sleeps

so his body blows up and floats.
    We nail our stakes in the yard

to keep him
    tethered to this world.

See how he splashes
    in summer when he knocks

his mouth against moon water.
    See how we paint with one finger

bright horses across his ribs,
    and rivers on the outside

streaming down his arms.

    ≈

Sometimes we sketch with smoke
    a door just over

that rock in our boy's chest. You can hear it
    rusty when he knocks

on our bedroom door to tell us
    he's been throwing up

for two months now
    like he saw his blood mom do.

We take the scent that falls from him—
    baby powder, gunpowder—

into our skulls because we live
    in an empty house,

and in each bedroom there's a bell
    ringing under the covers

where a child might live.

    ≈

We sledge the stake in our yard,
    then let the line out slowly

until our son's way up there
    where the moon makes

a lovely mess of him.
    When my wife and I

are overwhelmed with this,
    we beat our skulls upon the moon,

and it empties over the earth.
    I tell you, when we kiss,

even the little bell in my love's neck
    jingles, it rhythms,

it makes a lovely sound.